THE Rungawilla Ranger

Written by Dan Vallely Illustrated by Trish Hart

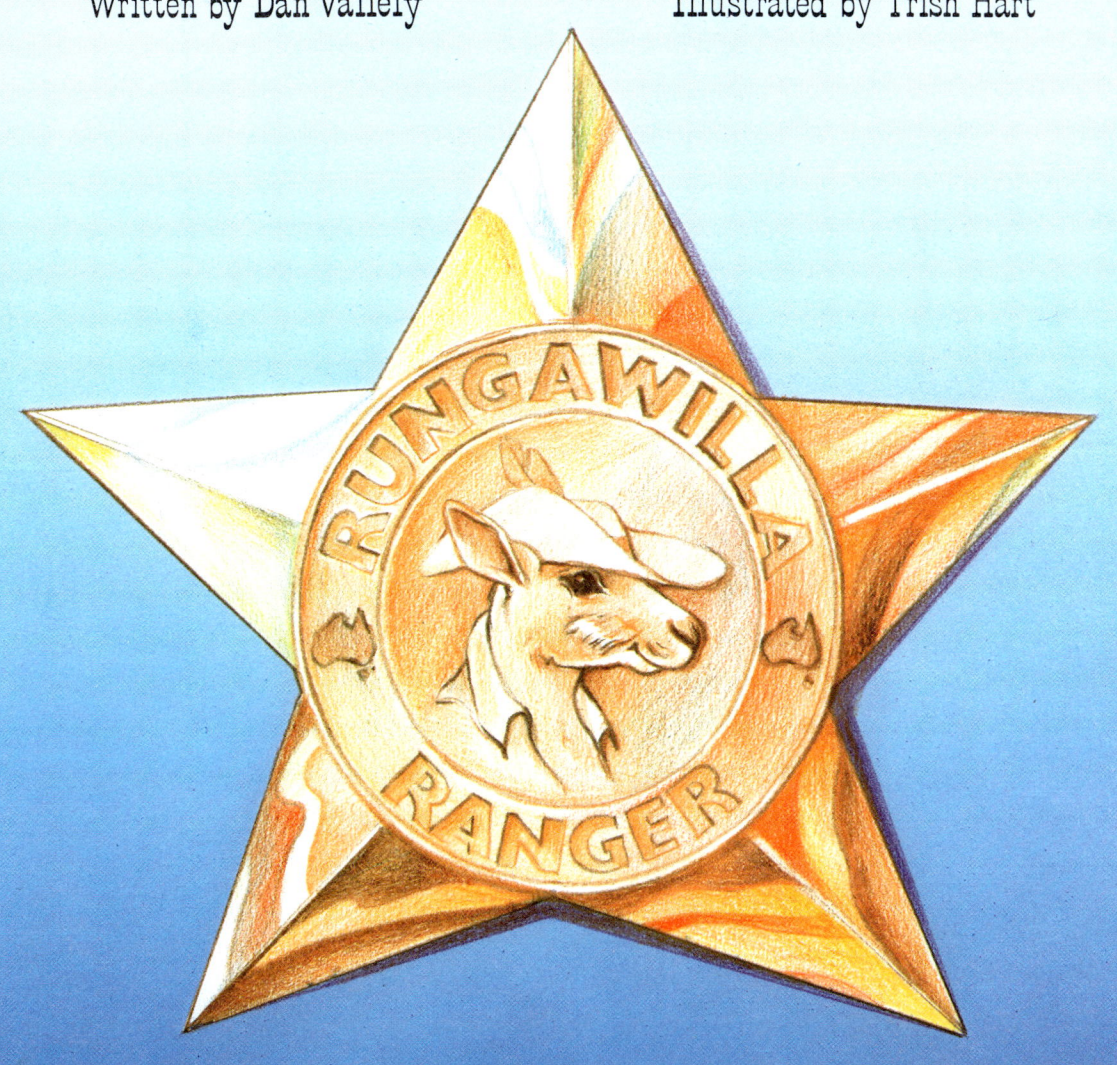

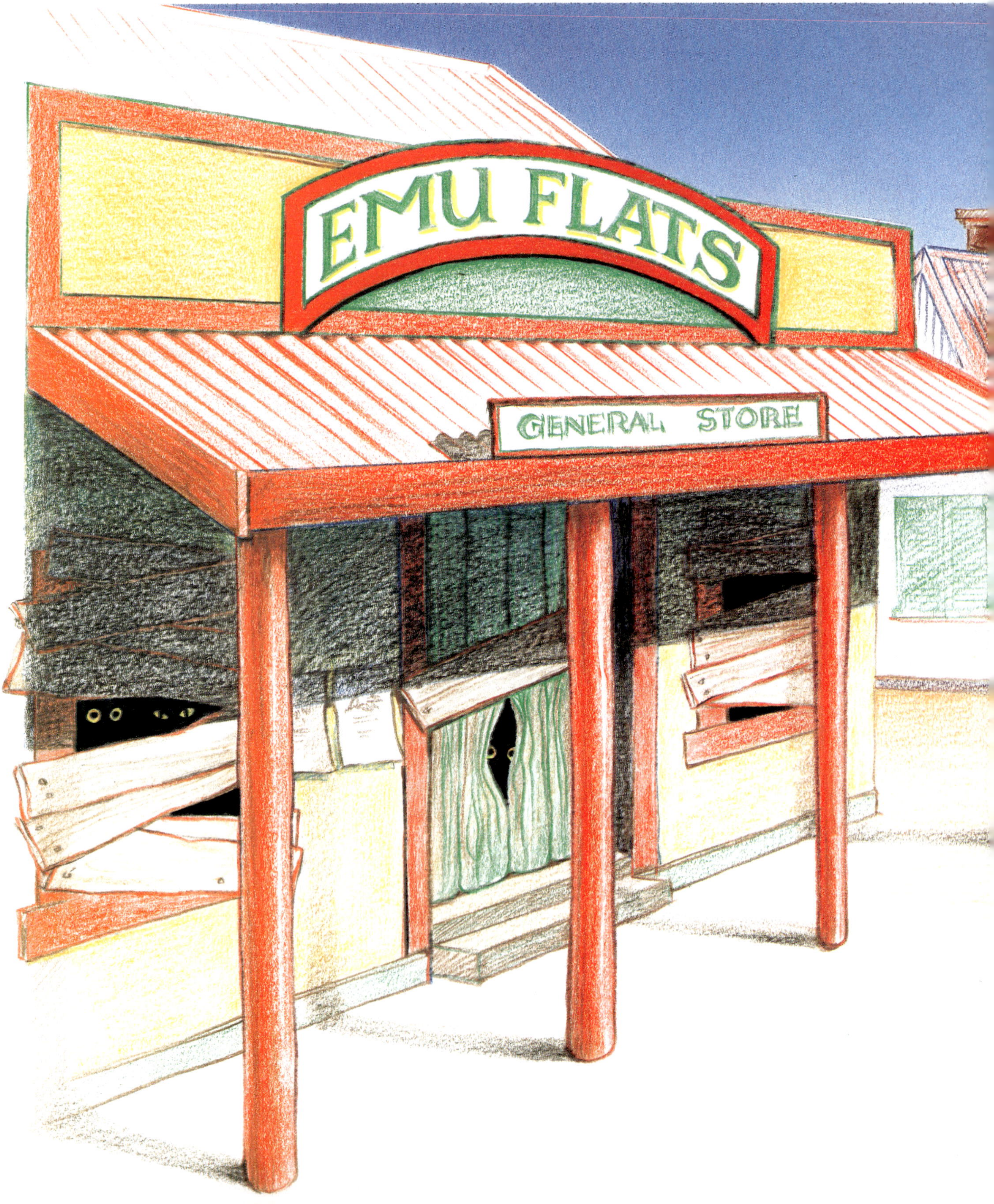
EMU FLATS
GENERAL STORE

The town was barred and shuttered,
For the word had got around —
Two bushrangers of ill repute
For Emu Flats were bound.

"Butch 'Chidna and Koala Kid
Are names that conjure fear,"
Said a pale and trembly wombat,
"And it's plain they're coming here!"

WANTED

KOALA KID

WANTED

BUTCH ECHIDNA

"They'll steal all our possessions!
Everything that isn't nailed!
They'll smash our town to smithereens!"
A nervous numbat wailed.

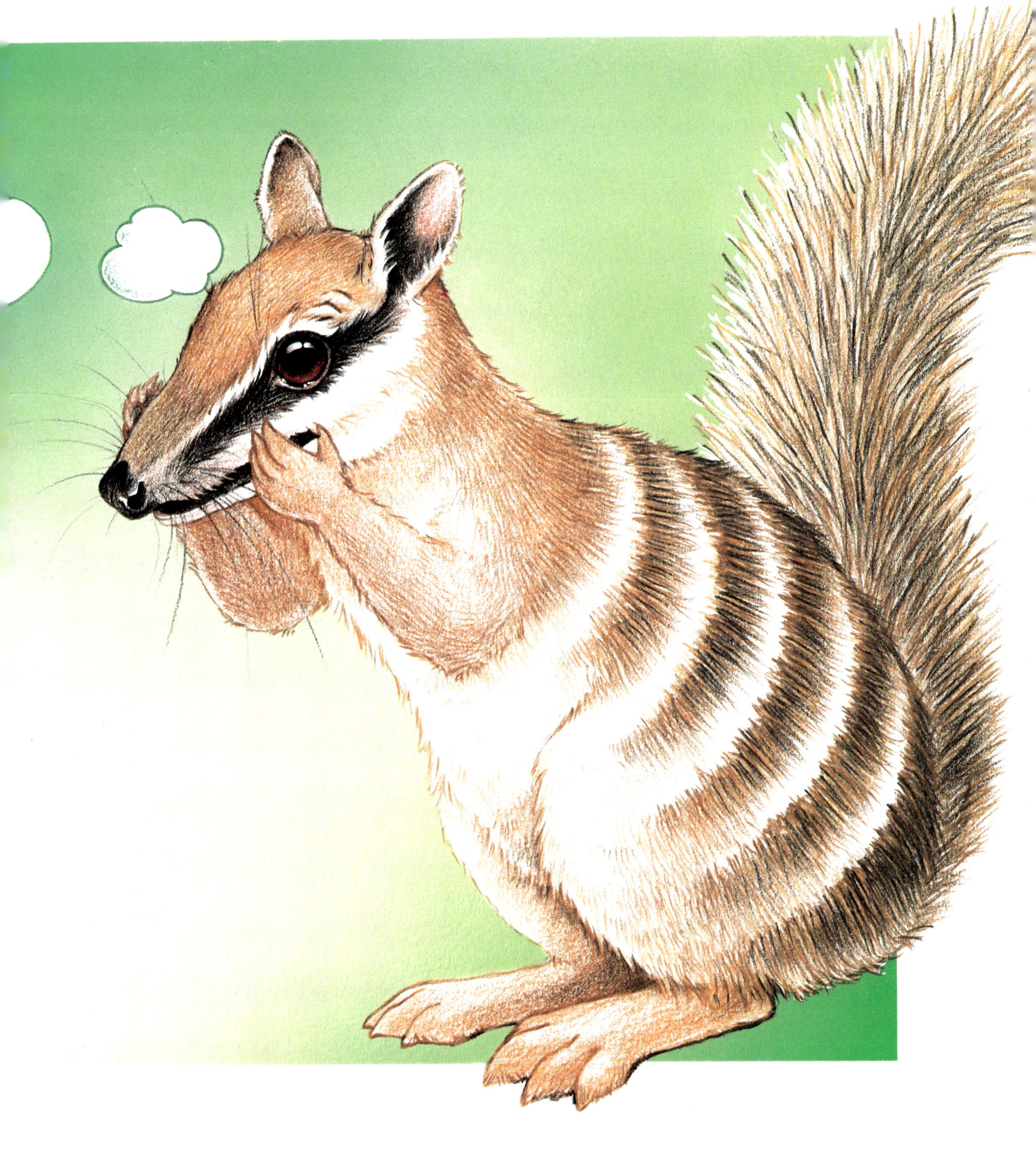

"Relax, my friends," a voice rang out,
"I've come to save the day.
For catching robbers such as these
Is how I earn my pay.

TRISH HART

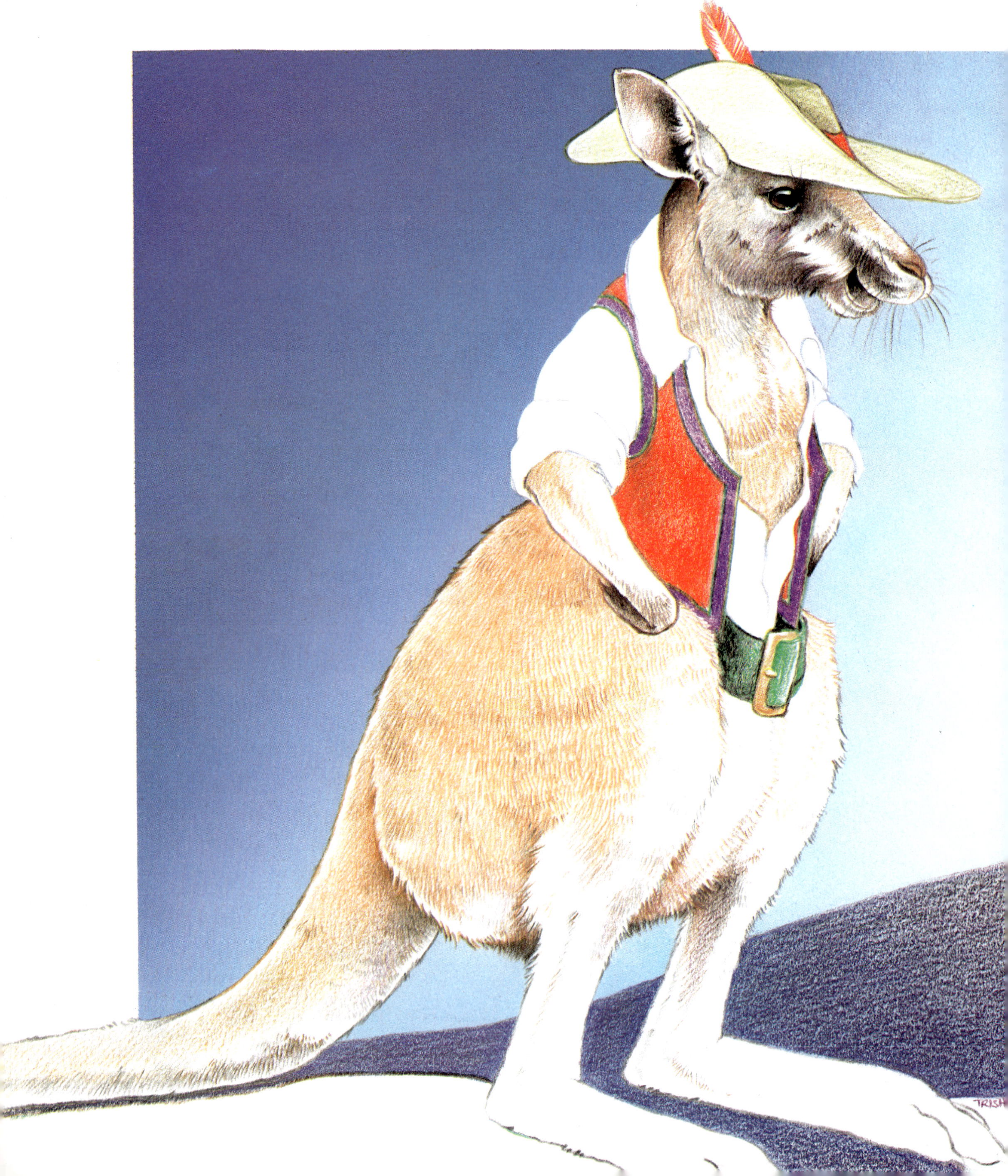
TRISH

"You may have heard of me before —
They call me Queensland Red."
They turned to see a handsome 'roo,
Slouch hat upon his head.

Huge muscles bulged beneath his shirt;
His eyes were cold and keen;
The scars of many battles
On his fur were clearly seen.

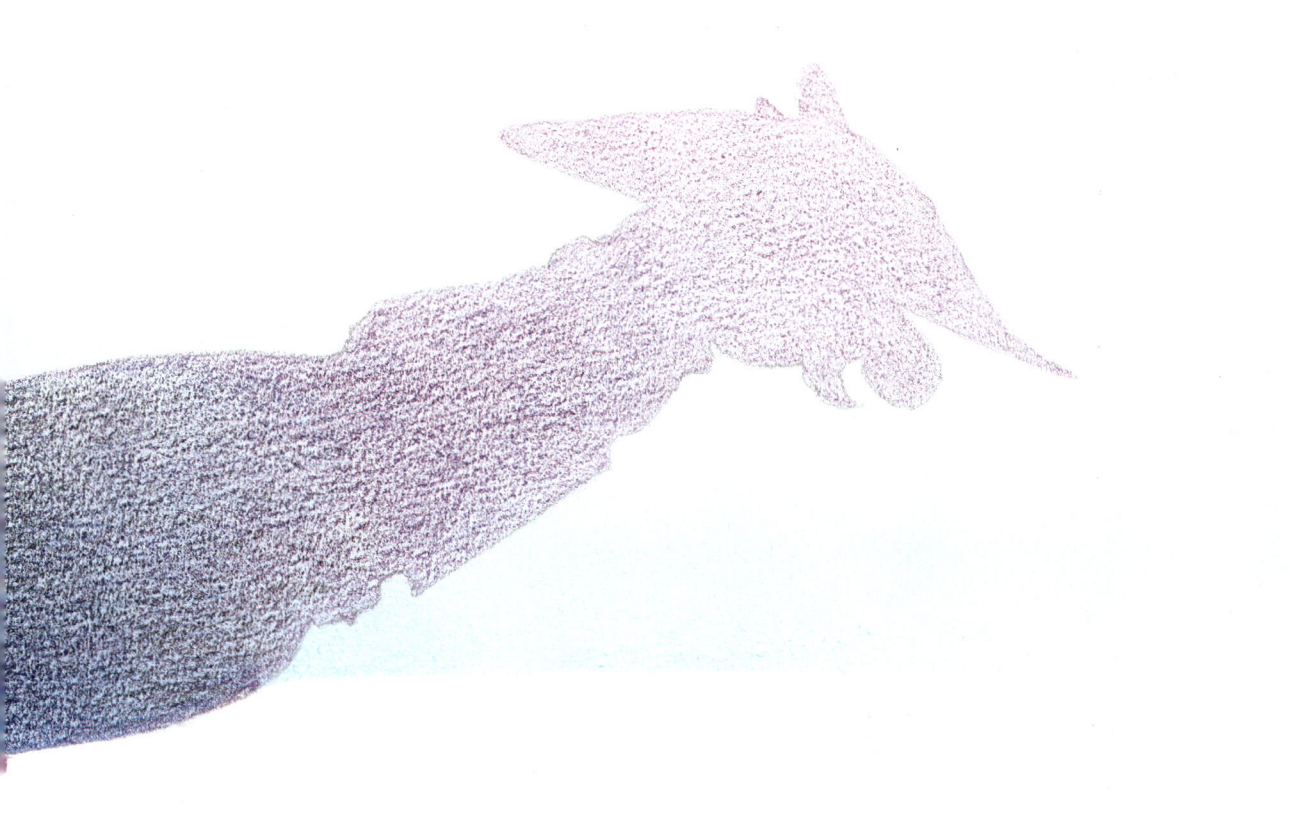

A storm was fast approaching
As they rode in from the East —
Each evil-smelling outlaw
On his evil-tempered beast.

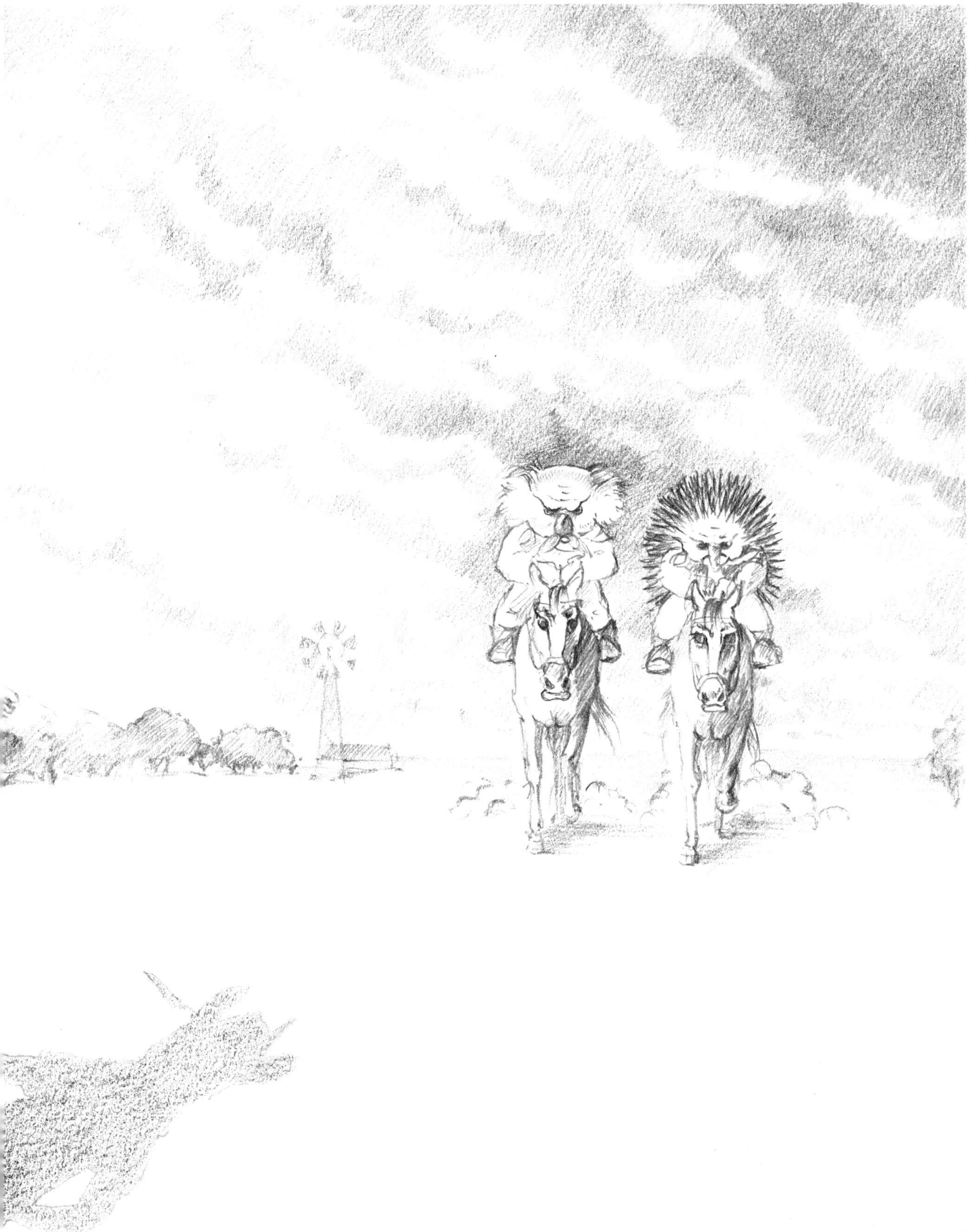

The air was charged with tension
As the Town Hall clock struck noon.
Echidna gave a mocking laugh —
And went for his balloon!

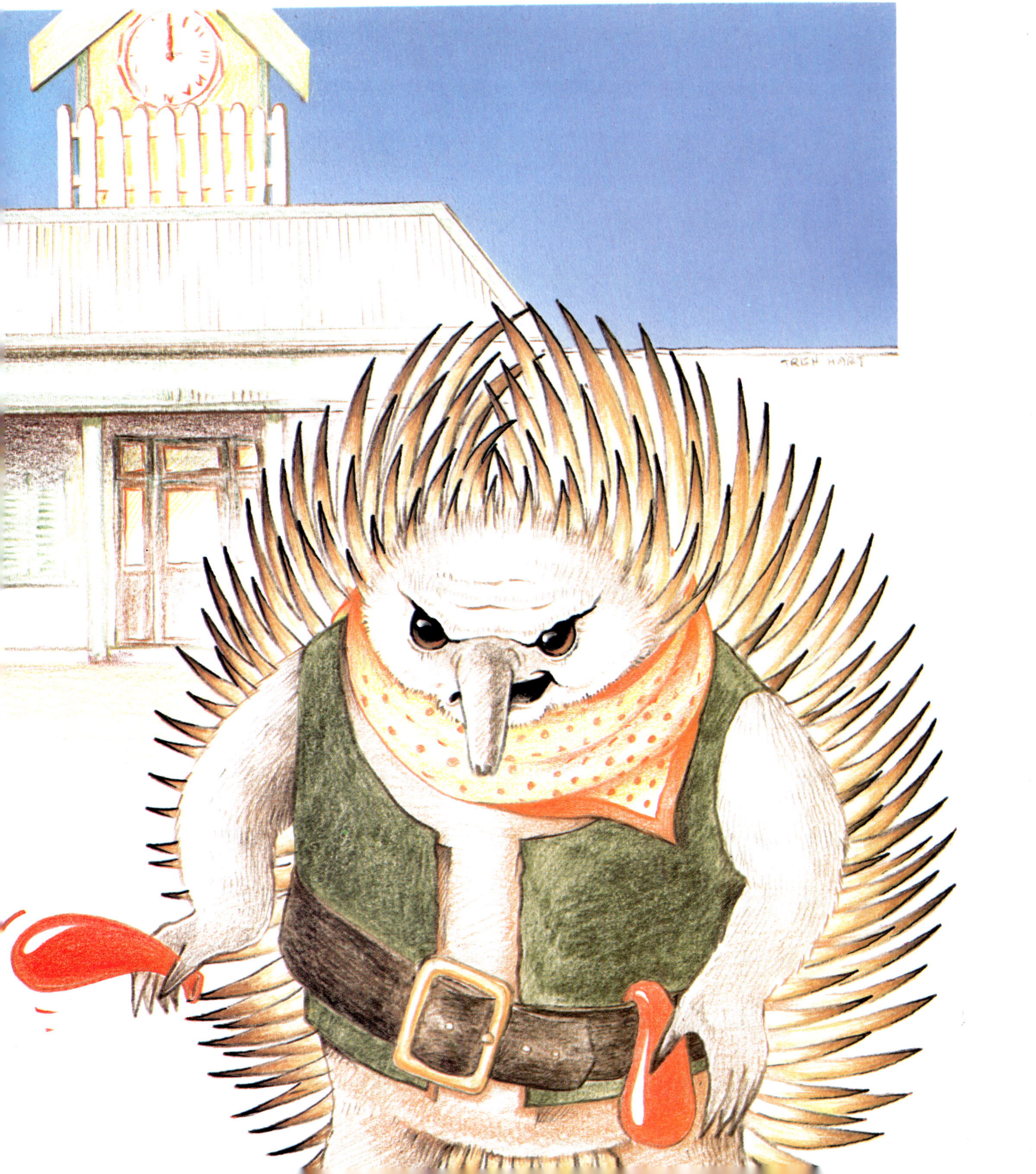

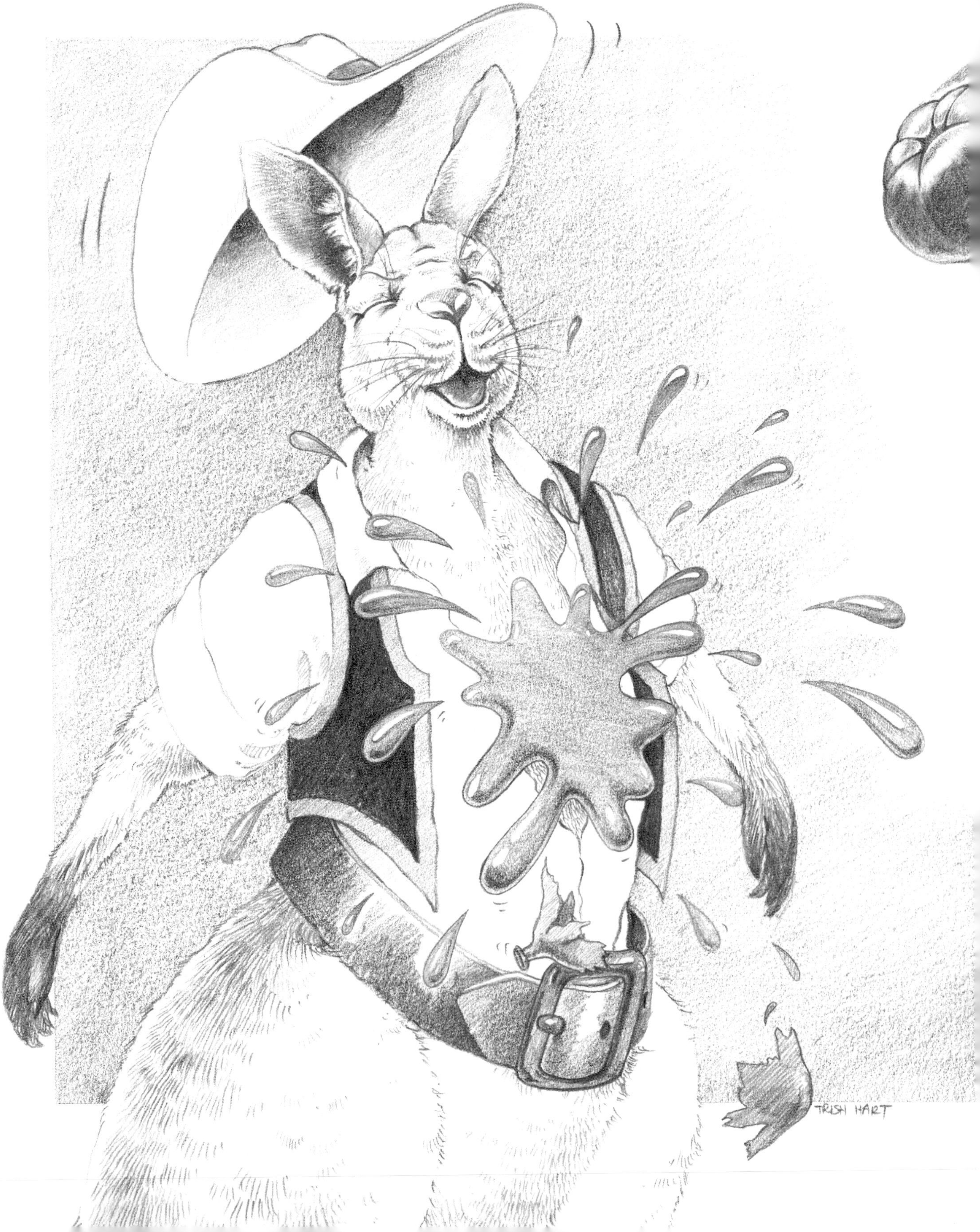
TRISH HART

With deadly aim it flew and burst
Upon the lawman's chest,
Discharging scarlet paint
Upon his silk embroidered vest.

He staggered back bespattered
From the cowardly attack —
Koala Kid's tomato
Biffed him with an awful thwack.

But Big Red's draw was lightning,
And a dreaded custard pie
Cleared leather, flew and splattered
Into Butch Echidna's eye.

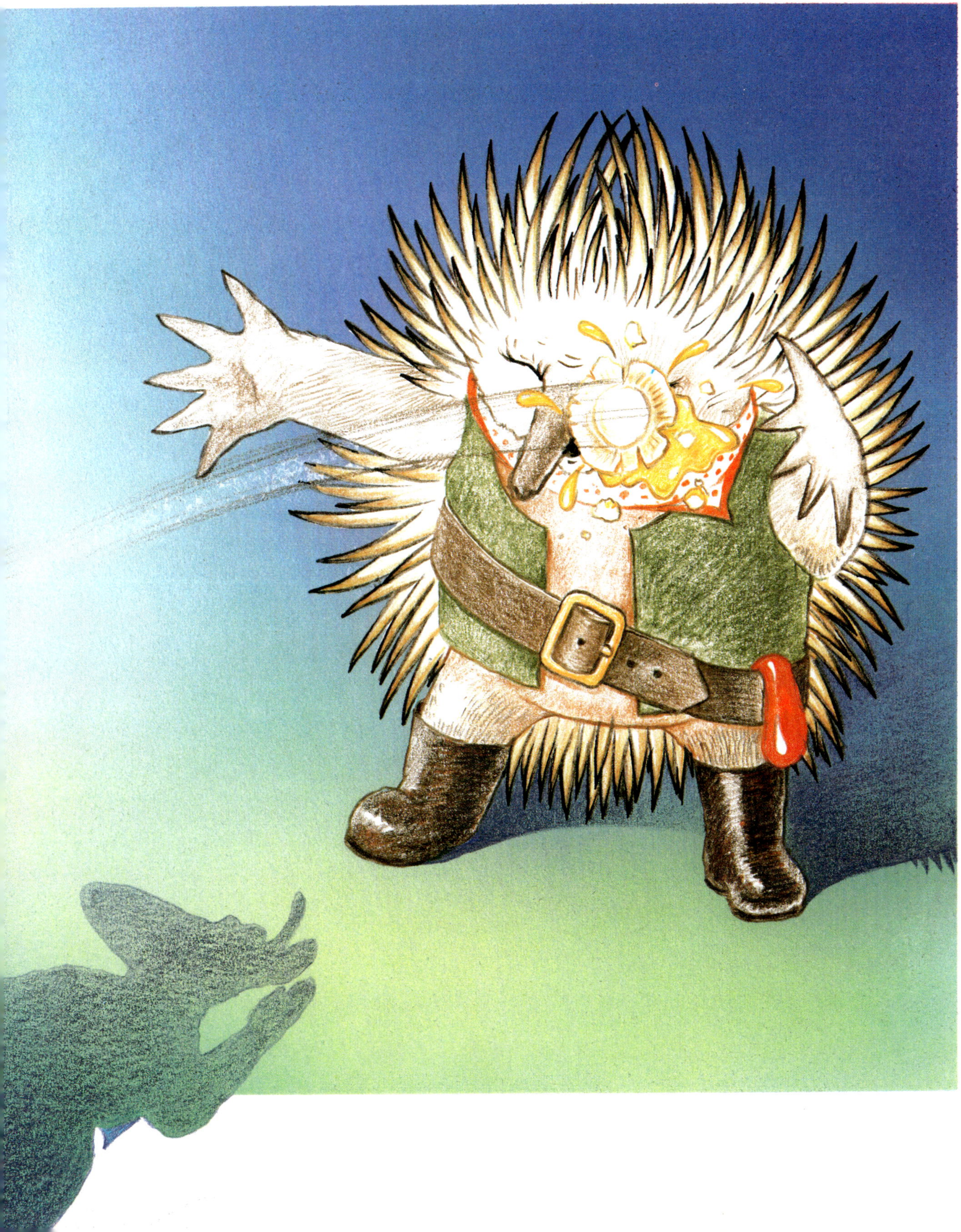

The outlaw stooped with strangled oath
To claw away the crust —
A rotten orange found its mark —
Echidna bit the dust!

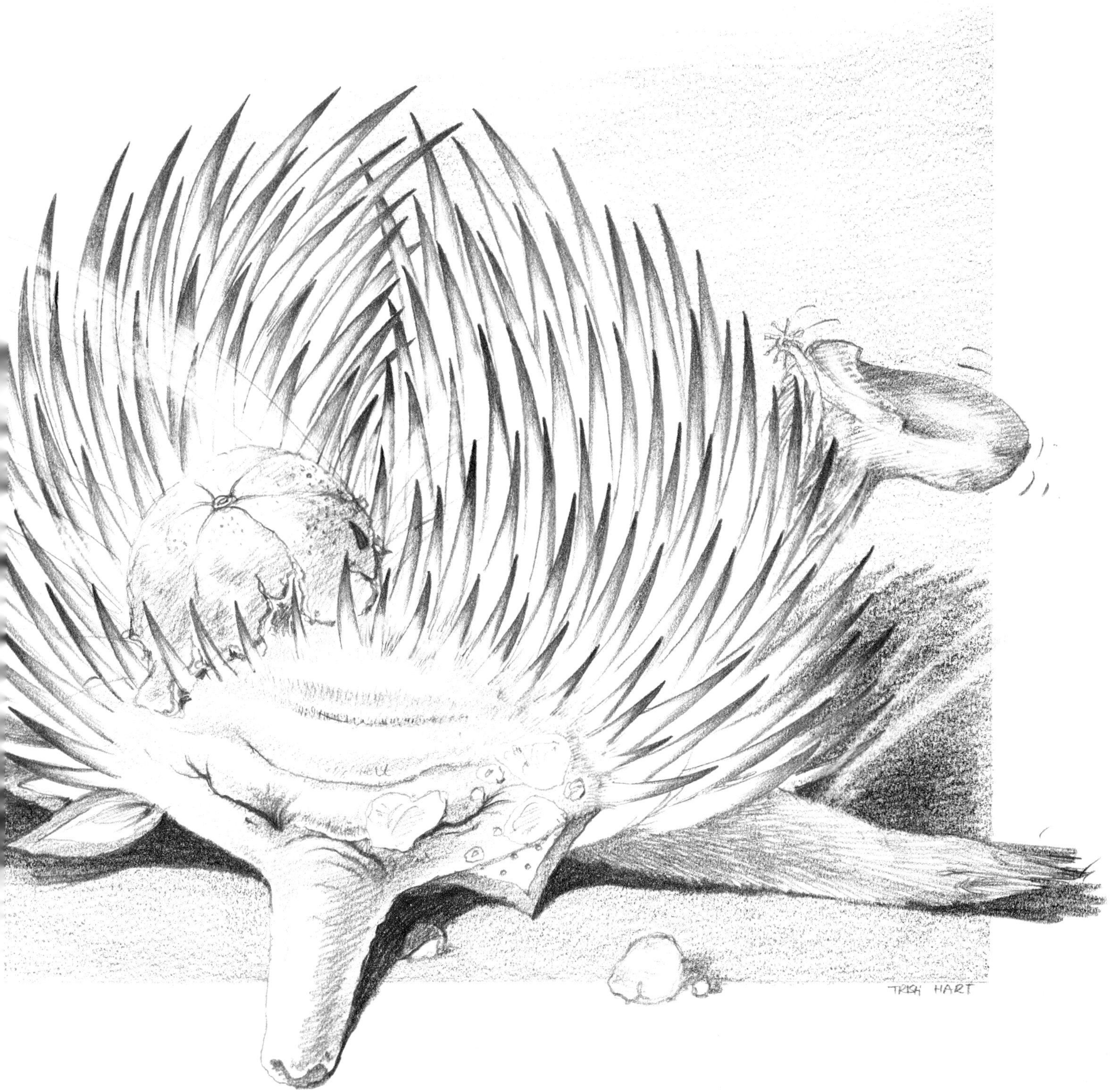
TRISH HART

With fear upon his cruel face
The Kid jumped on his horse,
And through the jeering onlookers
His way began to force.

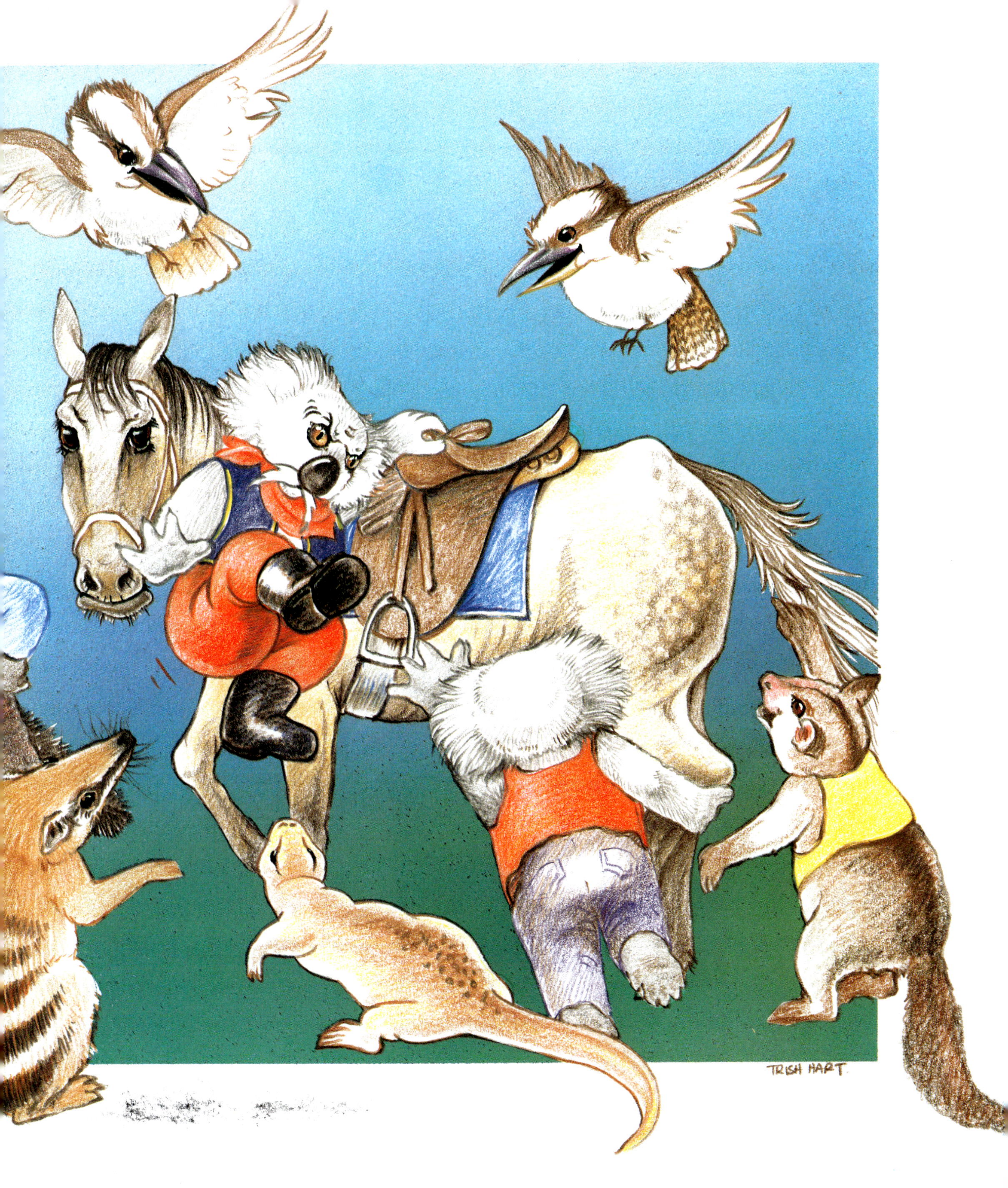
TRISH HART

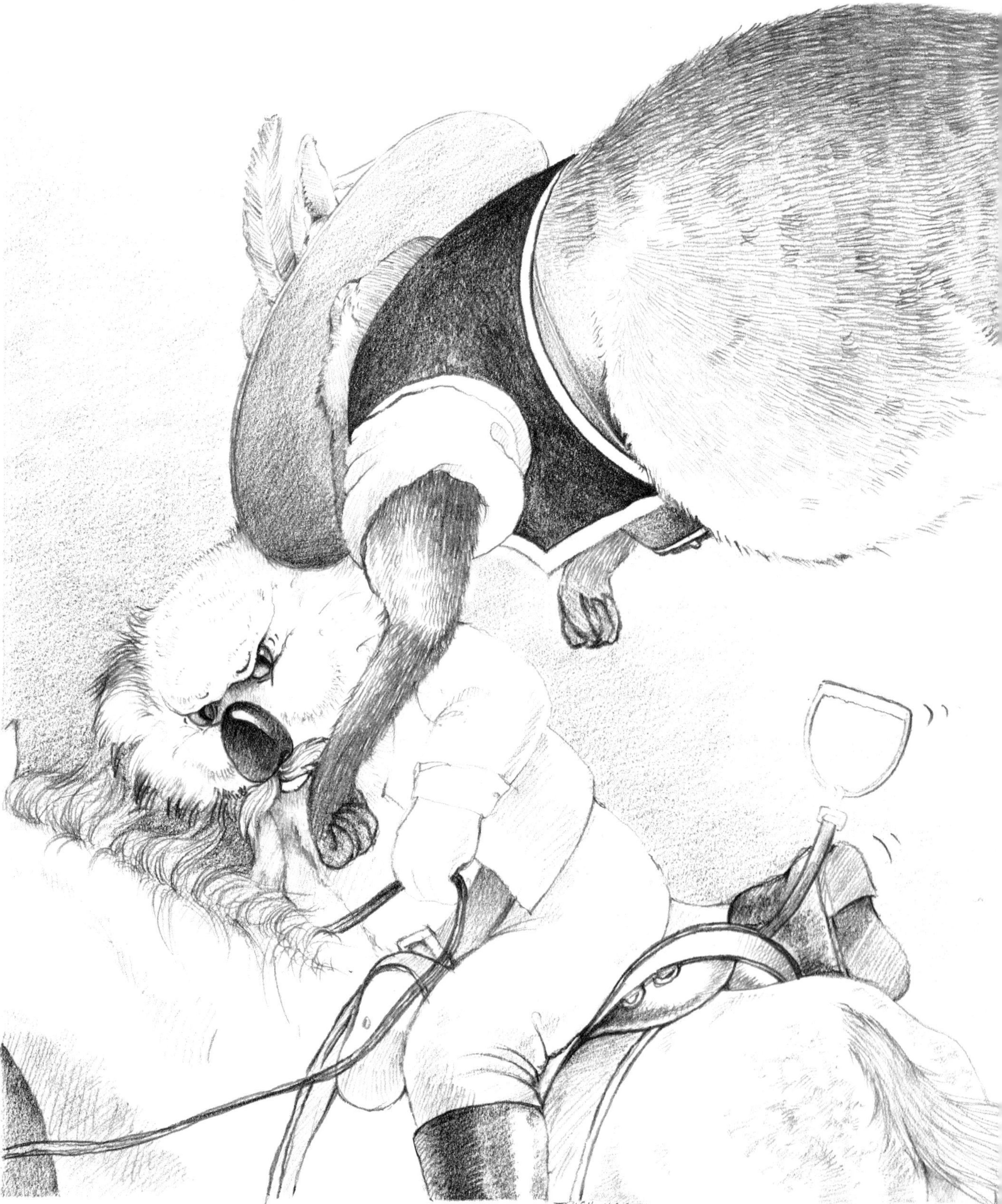
TRISH HART

But Red jumped high — a mighty leap
That surely did astound!
He grabbed the snarling Kid
And brought him crashing to the ground.

Echidna, now recovered,
Vowed he'd make the lawman pay,
And blows and kicks were traded
In the wildest country way.

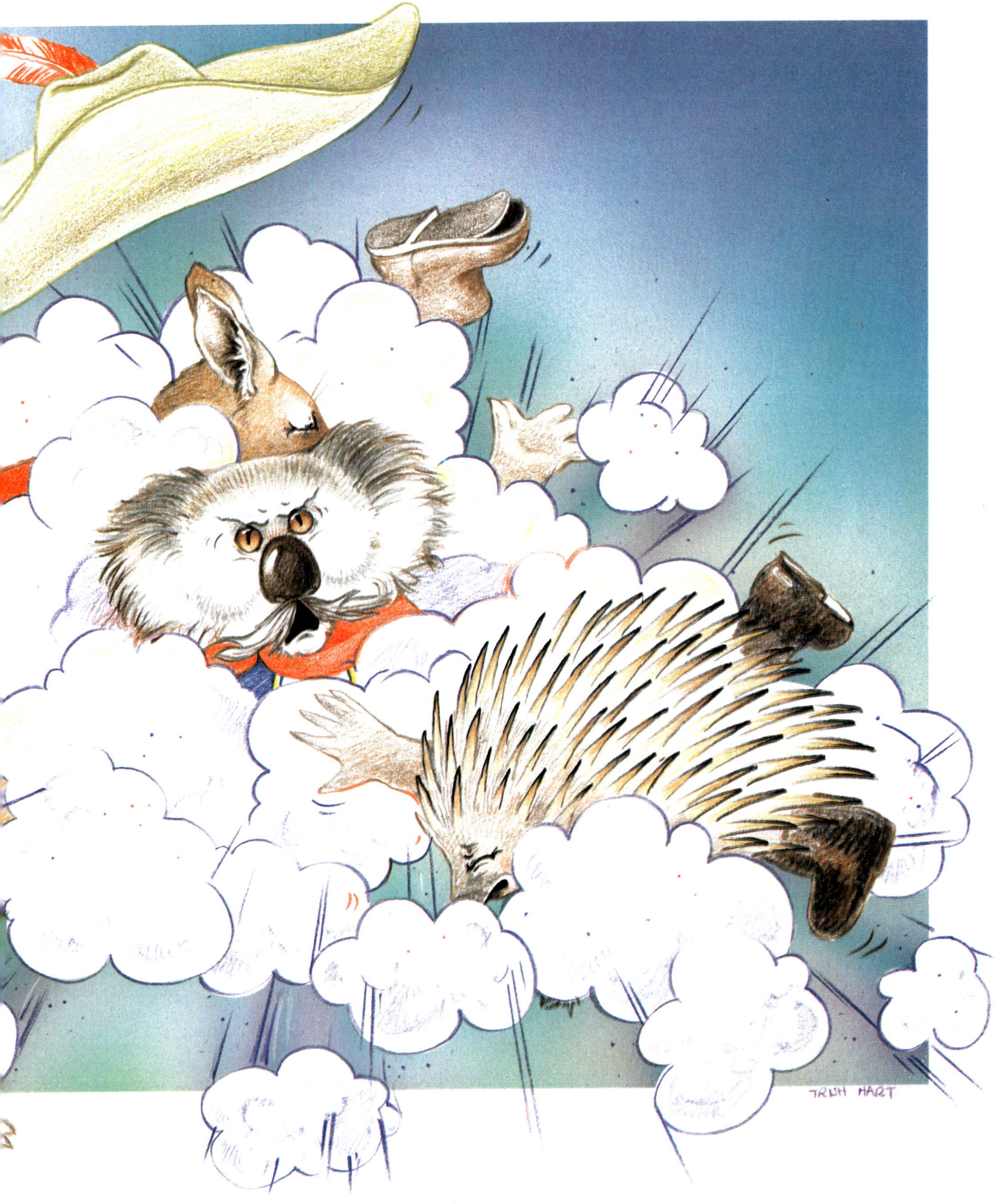
TRISH HART

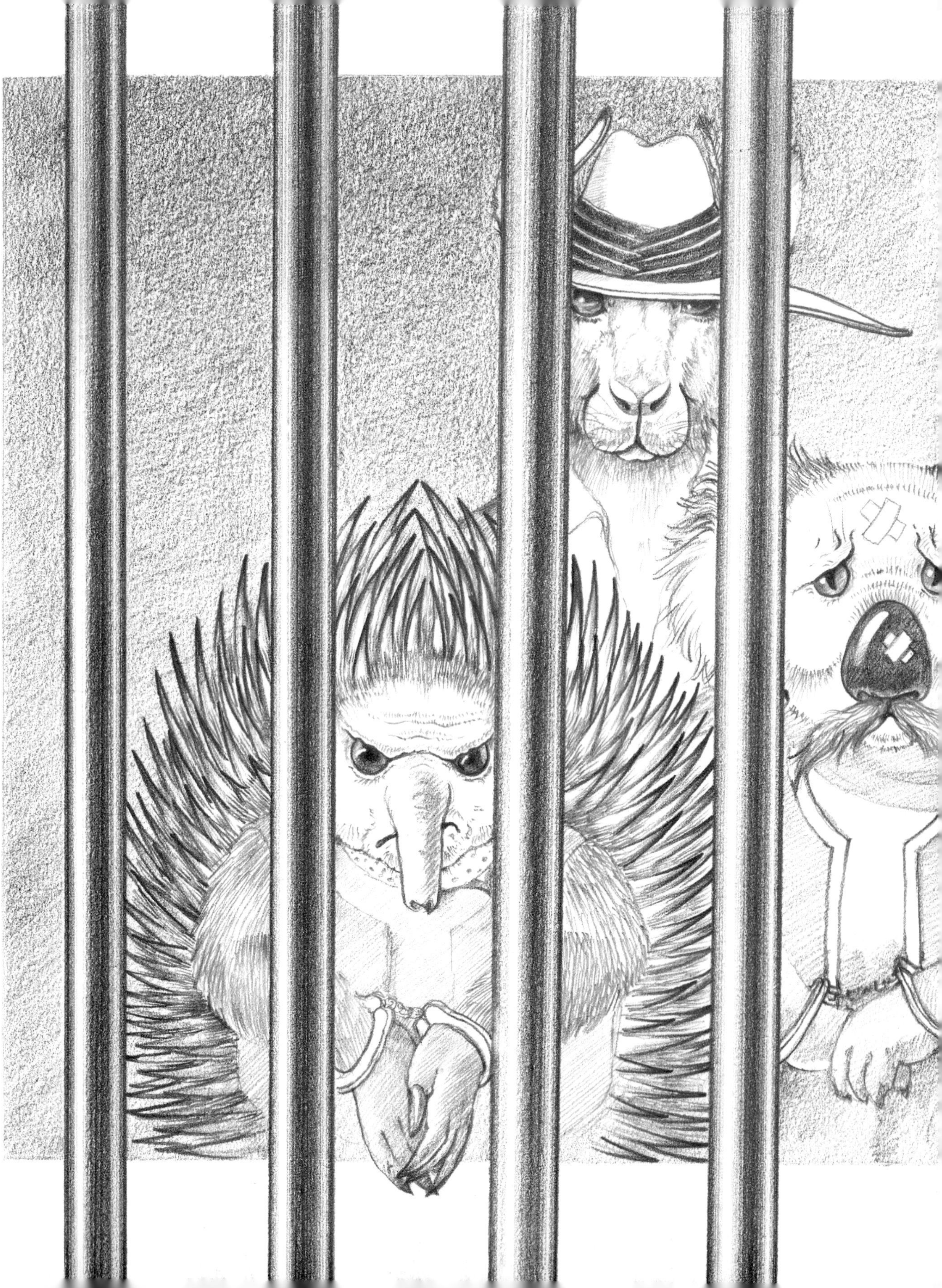

But fighting heart and courage
Saw the gallant 'roo prevail.
And two exhausted baddies
Made a weary trek to gaol.

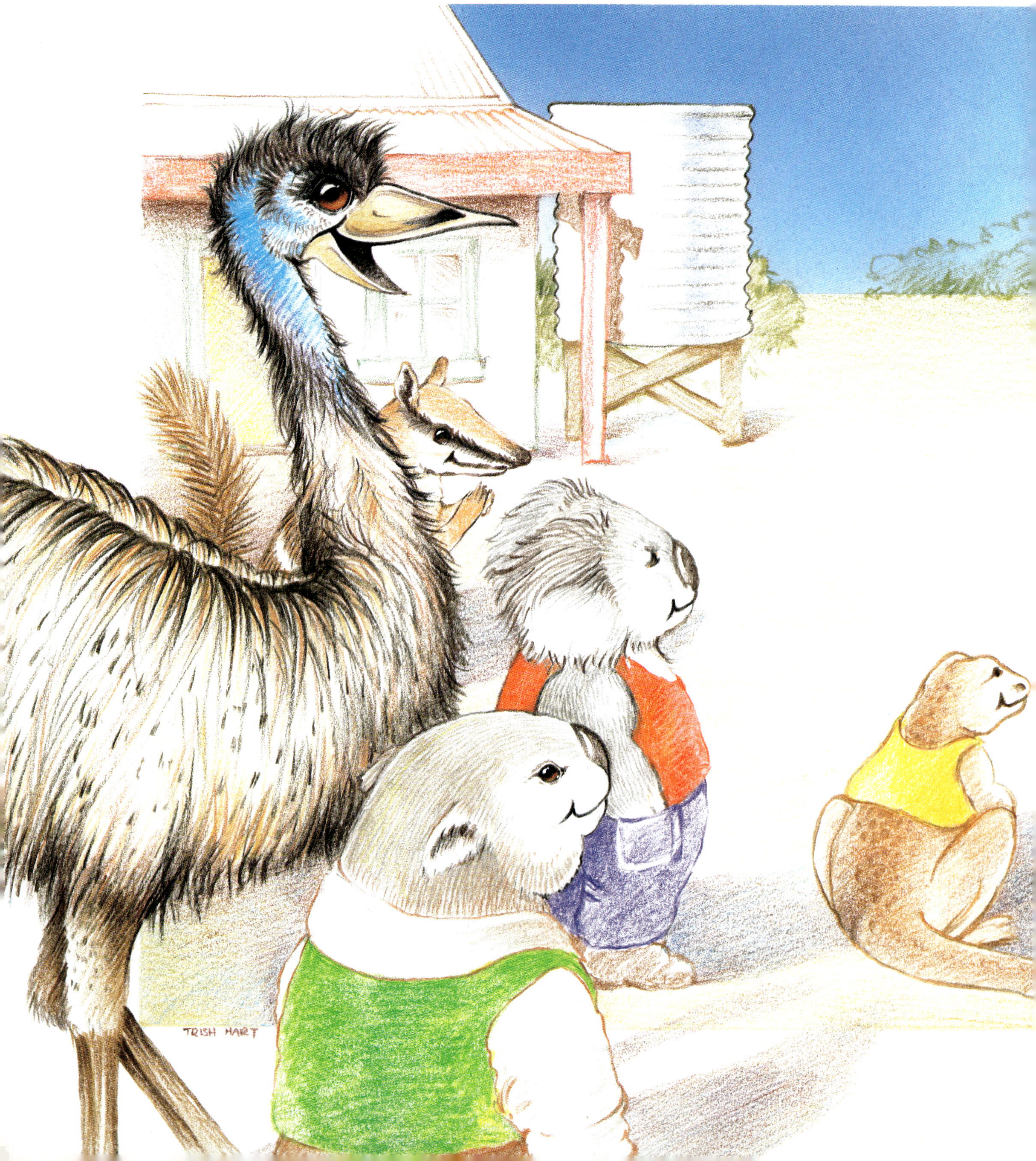
TRISH HART

As Red rode off an emu said,
"The 'roo that laughs at danger,
The hero of the bush —
Why, that's the Rungawilla Ranger!"

ANGUS & ROBERTSON PUBLISHERS

Unit 4, Eden Park, 31 Waterloo Road,
North Ryde, NSW, Australia 2113, and
16 Golden Square, London W1R 4BN,
United Kingdom

This book is copyright.
Apart from any fair dealing for the
purposes of private study, research,
criticism or review, as permitted
under the Copyright Act, no part may
be reproduced by any process without
written permission. Inquiries should
be addressed to the publishers.

First published in Australia
by Angus & Robertson Publishers in 1986
Reprinted 1987

Text copyright © Dan Vallely 1986
Illustrations copyright © Angus & Robertson
Publishers 1986

ISBN 0 207 15294 2

Typeset in 12pt Bookman Light by
The Type Shop
Printed in Singapore